HAPPY BUDS: MARIJUANA FOR ANY OCCASION

Copyright © 2011 Quick Trading Company
Published by Quick American Publishing
A division of Quick Trading Company
Piedmont, CA
Printed in China

Executive Editor: Ed Rosenthal
Content Contributors: Anna Foster, Mamakind
Additional Contributors: Ames Beezer, Ethan Sommer, Minda Quickel
Editors: Angela Bacca, Jack Jennings
Art Director: Hera Lee
Cover and Interior Design: Alvaro Villanueva

Photo Credits:
ArtOk p. 4, p. 21; Alvaro Villanueva p. 15, p. 55, p. 58, p. 104; Joe Burull p. 33, p. 34, p. 75; Cheba Hut p. 43, p. 143; Jenny Rollo p. 65; Ed Rosenthal p. 59, p. 73; Sannie's Seeds p. 83; Josh Word p. 41.

Courtesy of/Special Thanks to:
Bambu®Apparel p. 4, p. 21; Medi-Cone p. 15; seedleSs clothing Co. p. 41; Bhang Chocolates p. 58; Vapor Brothers, Volcano Vaporizer, Essential VAAAPP™ pg 86.

Publisher's Cataloging-in-Publication
(Provided by Quality Books)

    Rosenthal, Ed.
        Happy buds : marijuana for any occasion : dance, play, chill, snuggle /
        Ed Rosenthal ; with Anna Foster and Mamakind.
            p. cm.
            Includes index.
            ISBN-13: 978-1-936807-07-9
            ISBN-10: 1-936807-07-6
            ISBN-13: 978-1-936807-42-0
            ISBN-10: 1-936807-42-4

            1. Marijuana. 2. Cannabis. 3. Emotions.
            I. Foster, Anna. II. Mamakind. III. Title.

            HV5822.M3R67 2011   362.29'5
                                QBI11-600108

HAPPY BUDS

Marijuana for Any Occasion

Dance · Play · Chill · Snuggle

ED ROSENTHAL
with Anna Foster and Mamakind

QUICK
AMERICAN

"Sun went down in honey
 And the moon came up in wine
 You know stars were spinning dizzy
 Lord the band kept us so busy
 We forgot about the time"
                    -from "Lazy Lightning"
                    by John Barlow,
            Courtesy of the Grateful Dead

Contents

HERBAL MEDITATIONS

WAKE 'N' BAKE

WORKING IT

HITTIN' THE SACK

THE HOLIDAZE

Introduction

For many of us, marijuana is an accompaniment to our lives, an accessory. Whether we are relaxing with friends, watching a movie, hiking or working at routine or complex tasks, we are likely to be affected by the THC circulating in our bodies. What was once a "vice" has become a way of life.

Just as you wouldn't wear the same clothes to work in the garden as you would when you go to a party, you want to prepare your brain with the right mood enhancer for the occasion.

That's what this book is all about. Finding the right variety to use for the road ahead or perhaps the place you are in; to make life more relaxing or more exciting and definitely more pleasurable.

Whatever the situation, it's covered in *Happy Buds*. From the morning wake 'n' bake to evening travels into dreamland (and everything in between), whether you are working or playing, here are our suggestions for the right buds to enhance your adventures.

My research team has labored day and night to test these strains and determine how they are best utilized in everyday life. Thanks to their tireless and dedicated work subjecting themselves to the rigor these trials required, we are able to present to you the most comprehensive and scientifically sound guide to enjoying your high.

Now this information is available to you right here. Make good use of *Happy Buds*. The information inside will enhance your life!!

A Night Out

Getting a little stir crazy? Cabin fever got you down? Let your party animal out of its cage and embrace the darkness, the fun and the freedom that comes with getting out, getting high and getting down.

Tip:

When heading out for a sensi-fied night on the town, it is always a good idea to pre-roll your joints. That way, sneaking off to smoke is simple and trouble-free. Rolling dilemmas are avoided (wind, lack of flat surface, the embarrassment of having to roll in front of your friends when you're all thumbs, etc). Just pull out your trusty stash box, can, tube or saddlebag and light 'er up.

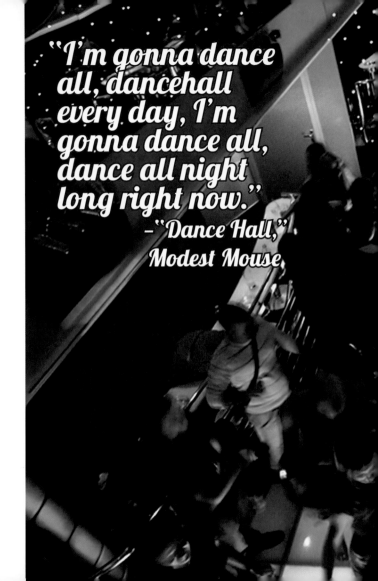

"I'm gonna dance all, dancehall every day, I'm gonna dance all, dance all night long right now."
—"Dance Hall," Modest Mouse

Dancehall

Dancehall is a pleasure for all the senses. The flavor mixes fruits with a green mossy flavor and a touch of haze, and lingers on the tongue in a satisfying way.

Dancehall is party weed that pairs well with a long night of dancing to irie Jamaican grooves. It has a progressive enduring effect that in-spires an alert, creative and sociable mood, perfect for getting up with the get down.

1st place 2010 Spannabis Cup

So You Don't Think You Can Dance?

Is your "dancing" limited to nodding your head to the beat? Hit the dance floor and the only move you can bust is the macarena? Throw these self-explanatory tracks onto your playlist and even the most chronic and chronically left-footed will be able to get down and funky.

Dance	Song	Artist
The Dougie	"Teach Me How to Dougie"	Cali Swag District
The Dutty Wine	"Get Busy"	Sean Paul
The Lean Back (a.k.a. The Rockaway)	"Lean Back"	Terror Squad feat. Fat Joe & Remy
The Tootsie Roll	"Tootsee Roll"	69 Boyz
The Stanky Leg	"Stanky Legg"	GS Boyz
The One-Two Step	"1, 2 Step"	Ciara

MK-Ultra

MK-Ultra has a thick, lingering aroma and a fresh pine-tree flavor that surprises with a lingering tongue-fizz, like a carbonated soda or a fizzing candy. This immediate, jolting rush is hypnotic; the extreme flavor and smell make this strain bad for a sneak-a-toke, but perfect for the party icebreaker. MK-Ultra's stimulant stone overcomes body fatigue from a long night of dancing, but is too intense for focused work.

1st place 2003 *High Times* Cannabis Cup

Tip:

Always put your pre-rolled booty inside a trusty stash container, preferably one that's air/light tight. This keeps things fresh and prevents pungent wafts of ganja goodness escaping into the atmosphere (a tremendous heat score). Great stashes include tubes with snap-top lids such as candy containers, doob tubes or tubes that held blunt wraps or cigars, metal cigarette cases and tiffin/film canisters.

Jock Horror

Jock buds are frosty and tight. The taste is floral with a tangy, sweet-sour haze edge. Jock Horror offers a classic sativa high—powerful and visual—with enduring legs. It's a good strain for going out dancing, enjoying time with friends, or just making something dull more tolerable and possibly entertaining.

EAR BUDS
Soma-licious

Soma-licious delivers pleasure to more than just the taste buds. While it's terrific for enhancing enjoyment of great music, it seems to make bad music sound much worse (a good thing for the discerning music-lover). The high evokes a serene yet luminous state of mind that seems to awaken a broad, almost philosophical sense of acceptance and love for what is. The stress of the modern world is swept away with this change in perspective. A little Soma-licious can make the path to kindness and patience easier to find. It is the kind of high that brings a smile and a good belly laugh.

Tip:

Stoner albums to listen to while you're getting ready to head out for the night:

Snoop Dogg – *Doggumentary*

Sublime – *40oz to Freedom*

The Flaming Lips –
Yoshimi Battles the Pink Robots

Bob Marley & The Wailers – *Legend*

Cypress Hill –
Greatest Hits from the Bong

Modest Mouse –
*Good News For People
Who Love Bad News*

Kyuss – *Welcome to Sky Valley*

KiD CuDi –
Man on the Moon: The End of the Day

Girl Talk – *Feed the Animals*

EAR BUDS
AK-47

The AK-47 buzz is immediate and long lasting with an alert but mellow cerebral effect. Known as a "one-hit wonder" this variety can be a little spacey. It is great for playing and listening to music or other social activities with friends.

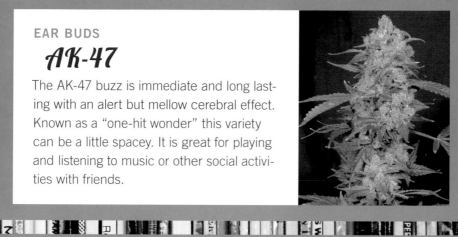

EAR BUDS
Titan's Haze

Titan's Haze brings back the legendary cerebral rush craved by sativa connoisseurs. The buzz soars with mildly trippy effects on heavier use, and a stimulating, creative impulse that endears it to artists and musicians. Use caution when mixing pleasures—combined with alcoholic beverages the potency may become unpleasant. Occasional users should show restraint to maximize enjoyment. More experienced sativa fans will delight in the ecstatic, clean, enduring high for this haze.

PARTY BUDS
Chiesel

This weed's flavors can serve as a party icebreaker, getting people talking, or circling for a taste of the hashy fuel pungency with a grapefruit sour edge. Chiesel energizes the party—this is a very up, energetic pot that has an electric enlivening feel to it. It leads to giggling and improvisational creativity, and it has enough body balance to bring out a sensual mood when the party is only for two.

Tip:

Inviting your dealer to your party almost always ensures free nuggage. Otherwise, it's quick and easy to have a buddy replenish the cannabis as coffers run low, keeping everybody happy and high—and you're the Man.

Arjan's Ultra Haze #2

This strain revealed THC levels at over twenty percent, so it's not surprising that Arjan's Ultra Haze #2 gives a very strong, fast and almost trippy high, with a well-balanced body vibration. Within the spectrum of haze highs, this one is on the fun, giggly side as it evens out. Absurdities and punch lines are everywhere when you smoke this strain, especially with like-minded friends. It is a terrific variety to enhance a bubbly or chatty mood for sparky social situations.

PARTY BUDS

Urban Poison

This is an urban brain safari. It has a cheerful alert quality that is great for energetic activities such as dancing. The up effect creeps into the consciousness and then through the body, with a long lifespan to the high. Many people find something special in the deep woodsy aroma and flavor that has just a touch of haze.

A Night In

Sometimes, there's no place like home—especially if you have some delicious buds to cozy up with. Break open your personal stash, grab your favorite paraphernalia, blankie, some comfort munchies, good company (or not), decide on the evening's entertainment and you're all good to…not go. Baby, it's cold outside…so warm yourself by the fire in your bowl.

Tip:

Want to be around people but don't feel like leaving the house? Try an online stoner chat room; meet interesting people locally and from around the globe, enjoy tokes together, chat about strains you like and join in interesting and varied conversations (most not even about pot), all without having to leave your buds at home or change your underwear.

Master Kush

Easy on the lungs and palate, Master Kush is non-expansive and smooth to smoke, giving an all-over body buzz that is both relaxing and stimulating. The high can also create optically pleasing effects, making it a good candidate for taking in a movie or museum visit.

Kiwiskunk

Kiwiskunk has a great skunky taste with a touch of citrus. The smoke is sweet and bright with a light inhale. Don't be fooled. This skunk packs a punch! A bowl of Kiwiskunk will drop you into a deep stone with giggles inside it, best enjoyed from a sofa in front of a big-screen movie.

Tip:

Stoner movies and documentaries to enjoy whilst tripping the bud fantastic:

The Union:
The Business Behind Getting High

Jay and Silent Bob Strike Back

Smiley Face

Super High Me

Pineapple Express

Grandma's Boy

Half Baked

How High

Harold & Kumar Go to White Castle

Up In Smoke

The Big Lebowski

Dazed and Confused

CINEMATIC BUDS
Killing Fields

Killing Fields delivers big dense buds that have a flashy, spacey, creeper high with a flavor of sweet-spicy overripe berries. The buzz is lucid and cerebral. It is highly functional for daytime or social activities, yet it can also help your concentration with the task at hand, remaining alert and engaged.

CRAFTY BUDS
Satori

In Japanese, "satori" means a moment of enlightenment in daily life. Satori's aromatic honey-herbal smoke has a fresh tinge that evokes thyme, oregano, and pine. The variety aids to access those bliss moments when seeing, knowing, and loving the world are the same. It is recommended for consciousness-expanding experiences and artwork.

DIY Memo / Photo / Roach Clip

The beauty of this clip is that its naughty side is easily camouflaged by clipping a picture of a puppy, or your grandma, or your grocery list to it and sticking it on your desk (a good way not to lose your dealer's number, too).

Materials

Thread spool (wood is the nicest to look at, but plastic will work)

Alligator clip

Heavy picture-hanging wire

Tape

Hot glue and gun

Pliers

Wire cutter

Optional: paint, sparkles, pictures— anything you'd like to decorate your clip with

Method

Cut wire to desired length. Three to five inches usually works. Use pliers to crimp the alligator clip to the wire. Tape off the hole on one end of the spool. Fill the open end with hot glue. Put the wire all the way into the hole; wipe off excess glue and hold wire steady until the glue cools. Paint, bedazzle and otherwise decorate your clip to your liking.

New York City Diesel

Soon after the exhale, bygones will become bygones and clouds of obsessive hard feelings will be broken up by rays of sweet creative energy. NYC Diesel is a cerebral daytime toke with a hint of body stone, good for recreation and making or enjoying art.

PolarLight

PolarLight's aroma has delicious notes of fruity-sweet and some spice with hints of haze. The genetic heritage gives a great sativa stone that will appeal to haze enthusiasts. This is a clear, cerebral, and energetic high, a lasting experience that may seem to soar ever higher over its duration. PolarLight is a good strain to get the creative juices flowing.

Tip:

Always have a healthy assortment of food you enjoy around. When the munchies hit at night, you won't have to hit the gym for the next week of mornings to make up for it. Popcorn, granola, fresh fruit and veggies, nuts, cheese—choose foods that take a while to enjoy and are fun to eat. Hemp is a healthy, hearty and very tasty additional ingredient to everything. Take advantage of your heightened senses of touch, smell and taste.

Cannabis Blue Cheese Dip with Fresh Veggies

Gather an assortment of your favorite veggies: carrots, celery, cucumber, broccoli and dip into Cannabis Blue Cheese Dip for a tasty, tainted snack.

Ingredients

½ cup melted (Aunt Sandy's 10X) cannabutter

¾ cup Ranch dressing

1 tbsp hot pepper sauce

¼ tsp cayenne pepper

¾ cup blue cheese, crumbled

½ cup sour cream

3 tbsp milk

Instructions

Combine all ingredients in a mixing bowl. Whisk thoroughly until well blended and sour cream is a smooth consistency. Makes 2 ½ cups

**Recipe from *Aunt Sandy's Medical Marijuana Cookbook: Comfort Food for Body and Mind* by Sandy Moriarty.

AMS

The AMS high is gradual. It spreads slowly within the body, heightening until it reaches its apex, then dissipating rather quickly. The body effect is smooth and relaxing with a deep muscle effect, making it a successful choice for those with multiple sclerosis or insomnia. AMS is a smoke for winding down and kicking back, rather than kicking off the party. To maximize the enjoyment of this strain, have a nice toke before a massage, or take a puff from the vantage point of a lounge chair on the deck after the week's work is done.

"Only your real friends will tell you when your face is dirty."
–Burmese proverb

Burmese Kush

The BK buzz is a creeper, but when it arrives, the feeling is calming and brings in a centered sensation rather than a big gong to the head. It is good for those that prefer a mellow high instead of a heart-racing speedy sensation. Her aroma and flavor is great for both jet setting and for relaxing and enjoying a leisurely meal once you've arrived at your destination. Burmese Kush's genetic makeup suggests medical applications for pain relief and appetite enhancement.

Vanilluna

Vanilluna possesses flavors that are smooth and creamy, with a sweet vanilla taste and a hint of floral bouquet and sweet melon musk. The experience is top-shelf quality, with a comfortable entry and an enduring dreamy effect that induces calmness and clarity. It's a good variety for relaxation and reducing anxiety, a tasty treat for the palate and a bubble bath for the nerves.

Fun In the Sun

There is no better way to enjoy the great outdoors than while enjoying one of Mother Nature's greatest gifts—the cannabis plant. With sun on your face, wind in your hair and herb in your pocket, you're ready to take on the elements with red eyes and a smile. Whether climbing among the kushes in the Himalayas, or barbecuing in your backyard in the suburbs, great weed makes the awesomeness of our planet even more fascinating and profound.

Pineapple Punch

Pineapple Punch's tropical spell is likely to leave you giddy. This is a great upbeat high that brings on lots of talking and grinning. It's a terrific accompaniment to an outdoor concert or a walk in nature. Pineapple Punch encourages a sunny perspective and offers a pick-me-up for recreational afternoons.

Sputnik

Sputnik has a strong stone with a kiss of well-being behind it. The variety's creator and well-known breeder, Subcool, recommends writing, thinking, talking, music and art as good activities while in Sputnik orbit. You may be more inclined to let your goofy side out to play.

Black Berry

Black Berry high is upbeat and clear, with a quick onset and a tapering endurance. It is a functional smoke well suited to daytime activities and creates a more casual, unhurried sense of well-being, without impairing one beyond comfort in most social situations. The flavor is heavy and fuel-like and forms thick smoke. The finish leaves hints of spicy South Asian flavor on the tongue.

Road Trippin'

When the yellow line calls, follow these road-worthy guidelines to make your diesel-fueled vehicular journeys as pleasant as your dank destinations.

1. **Have a plan.** Know where you're going, what the road conditions are and most importantly, if you have enough weed to get you there and back.

2. **Pre-roll all the joints you'll need** just for the current leg of the journey.

3. **Break only one law at a time.** Make sure your car and license are up to code and don't speed while holding—don't be overly cautious either, or you'll have a line of honking grannies behind you attracting heat. Air out the car after blowin' dro.

4. **Keep everything handy**—pre-rolled joints and everything you'll need in your trusty stash container. Check! Lighter, back up lighter, and disposable ashtrays (soda cans) within reach.

5. **Not flying solo?** Make sure your co-pilot or convoy is prepared with *S.W.I.M.*—Snacks, Weed, Info, Music.

S.W.I.M.

Snacks. Plenty of thirst-quenchers and napkins for clean up.

Weed. The Dream: providing the bud altogether. The Reality: packing bowls and keeping track of the stash, lighter, papers, etc. should suffice.

Information. Every Captain Kirk needs a Sulu and/or Mr.Spock. The navigator is responsible for: maps, directions, itineraries, reservations and taking care of the details.

Music. It's a good idea to agree on a playlist (before you head out), or a listening schedule of stations everyone agrees on. See chapter one for stoner album suggestions for the long haul.

"Casey Jones leanin' out the window,
taking a trip to the Promised Land"
–"Casey Jones," Johnny Cash

Fun In the Sun

Casey Jones

The flavor of Casey Jones is as outstanding as the high itself. The high is felt almost immediately and lasts a little over an hour. This strain has an "up" effect, with a vividly trippy, thought-provoking quality that can lead to mental wandering. Under its effects, one may feel a stronger sense of connectedness to oneself and others (especially if you're unfettered by clothes). It's good for creative activities that can benefit from an introspective mood and don't require intense right brain focus. It's less than ideal if you need to make plans, balance your checkbook or do other very linear (most likely clothing-required) activities.

Grandaddy Grape Ape

There is a potent, undeniable grape tinge to this plant's aroma and a sweet grape taste that lingers subtly on the tongue. For an indica, her buzz is surprisingly alert and energetic, rather than highly sedating. This is a good smoke for frolicking in the high meadows and skinny-dipping in the lake.

1st Place 2004 Inglewood Medical Cannabis Cup and Green Cup 2004 to 2006

Tip:

Pick the appropriate strain to enhance your hike or run, rather than causing you to lose the oomph to get started or finish. Be sure to take time to notice the sounds, scents and other details of nature usually overlooked. Wear sunscreen and drink plenty of water; dry mouth is a good reminder to keep hydrated, no matter the cause.

Tip:

You heard the smoking bear: prevent forest fires by packing your roaches in a portable ashtray or airtight container, or field stripping them. Field stripping is breaking the roach apart until all that's left is a sprinkling of ash and a tiny bit of paper that can be safely thrown to the ground. Rip up the bit of paper and filter into small pieces, so it will biodegrade faster.

NATURIST BUDS
NYPD (New York Power Diesel)

New York Power Diesel is a blissful, balanced and relaxing buzz great for a campfire. She's a treat to smoke, starting with a clear, enjoyable transition and bringing a mixture of earthiness and lemon zing over a recognizable deep note of diesel acridity. This buzz is calming, full of wonder and sensory awareness. It can enhance discernment and pleasure. You will notice food's subtle flavors, the delightful scents, sights and sounds of the outdoors. NYPD is a seductive aphrodisiac.

HAPPY BUDS

Tip:

Create an instant windshield anywhere when you bring along a lightweight pop-up tent. Not only does it provide a private rolling station away from the elements, you can zip `er up, then light `er up, creating the perfect portable hotbox.

Speed Queen

Speed Queen, although an indica, has a stimulating and balanced mind-body high that doesn't put you to sleep. Mandala refers to this strain as the "surfers' choice." Surfers are true connoisseurs who sample fine grass at the world's best surfing spots. They like to stay on their feet, on the board and at the bonfire. Speed Queen has a potent, sociable buzz that you can ride like a wave. The high comes on quickly and is pleasantly relaxing, yet leaves plenty of energy for enjoying a full moon party or just watching the ships roll in.

Super Lemon Haze

Super Lemon Haze is a superstar. The winning combination of lemon/lime pungency and strong, spicy haze background is undeniably delectable. The high begins with a strong and immediate physical sensation, followed by a cerebral sense of elation. This pot has a fizzy social side, bringing people out of themselves into a good-humored, giggly and vivacious mood. Although it ranges into the slightly dreamy, this is definitely an active, clear and emotionally uplifting buzz. It is best suited for recreational activities in sand and surf.

1st Place 2008 & 2009 *High Times* Cannabis Cup

G-13 Diesel

G-13 Diesel's flavor is sweet and skunky, with unpredictable notes of citrus and, of course, diesel. This hybrid's high starts in the head with a cerebral flight of ideas, but quickly works its way into the body for a long lasting stone. In many respects, G-13 Diesel offers the classic marijuana experience: a peaceful smile, a relaxed body and a renewed appreciation for tasty snacks. This is a smoke for sunny days and happy times with friends floating down a river in an inner tube or snorkeling in shallow waters.

Time Out!

Every once in a while, we all need a break from the chaos of life. Sometimes all it takes is a brief affirmation to center ourselves; sometimes a deep and mindful meditation is required to keep it real, without completely losing it. Pot has been a favorite vehicle of many spiritual paths throughout the ages, but you don't need to be a swami to find inner peace and grounding.

Tip:

Share a bowl or joint to take a heated discussion down a few notches and encourage a more open, honest and reasonable dialogue. They don't call it a "peace pipe" for nothing!

DelaHaze

The flavor is haze, with sweet fruity accents. The high is a creeper with a clear-headed transition. DelaHaze has an active, functional, mood-lifting buzz that avoids both heavy and sedating physical effects and the speedy or trippy mental quickening that some head highs induce. Instead, the sensation has a calm clarity, smoothing out the doldrums and lightening the spirit to engage a more positive state of mind. A mild and pleasant body relaxation effect is often felt after some time has passed.

SERENITY BUDS
Blueberry

The name is obviously related to the flavor, but also fits with the cool blue hues of the buds. The taste and aroma have the signature Blueberry taste. This top-quality high is a notable and pleasantly euphoric experience that lasts a long time. Blueberry smoke will not put you to sleep, but it may make you forget what you were going to do.

1st Place 2000 *High Times* Cannabis Cup

Tip:

Candlelight sets a beautiful visual mood and is easy on eyes that have been exposed to too much fluorescent light. Pick hemp-based candles, which clean the air as they burn and lend a sensual scent to the room. Keep them away from curtains or other flammables and keep them in your line of vision, so that you DO NOT FORGET THE CANDLES ARE THERE! Put them out each time you leave the room. Potheads need to be extra vigilant.

Mandala #1

The Mandala #1 high spreads in euphoric waves of creative inspiration. It may start dreamy and a little spacey, but quickly settles into a relaxed and motivated sensation, with no racing heart or other unpleasant side effects. This strain has the sweet fragrance of dried apples and the purple plants also incorporate raspberry and a touch of fresh mint. This strain is excellent for reducing anxiety and for its anti-depressive effects.

Tip:

When setting out on an extended spiritual journey, try eating your buds in a snack or drink like bhang. Bhang, an Indian drink, is traditionally made by boiling crushed marijuana leaf in water and milk for a few hours until the leaf turns mushy and is dry enough to roll into balls. Ingesting your marijuana can make for a long and sometimes more intense trip than if inhaled.

ENLIGHTENING BUDS
Durga Mata

Named for the powerful and revered Hindu Mother Goddess, Durga Mata represents the purity and strength of purpose residing within the divine essence of every being. In Hindu tales, Durga Mata carries the sword of truth, destroying demons, conquering ignorance and leading humans to enlightenment. Durga Mata brings out your inner philosopher. The aroma is herbal and spicy, with a taste like Turkish fruit. The buzz is potent and physically relaxing, but not sleep inducing.

"Invoke the Mother Terrible to help us annihilate within ourselves all negative forces; all weaknesses, all littleness."
–devotional prayer to Durga Mata,
Swami Chinmayananda

LSD

The LSD flavor mixes a slightly nutty and earthy palate, with a dank sweet muskiness. Best of all, LSD lives up to its name, delivering a vivid, euphoric experience that stands out from the typical indica stone. While the body high has depth, the strongest sensation is the super trippy psychedelia that blows the cobwebs out of the corners of your mind. This strain is great in a stimulating environment. Music, food and colorful imagery are all enhanced under its influence. However, overindulgence or overly hectic situations may cause a sense of being overwhelmed, so it can be good to stay somewhere that offers a sense of comfort and safety.

1st Place Indica 2008 *High Times* **Cannabis Cup**

ENLIGHTENING BUDS
The Third Dimension

Third Dimension's buzz is a sparkle added to the mundanc day, making everything softer and funnier. In moderation, this stone is clearheaded enough for daytime enjoyment. However, this weed is equivalent to a tropical cocktail—its light, fruity flavors can make you forget its potency, so it's easy to overindulge. The Third Dimension may enhance snacking and is likely to rev up the imagination.

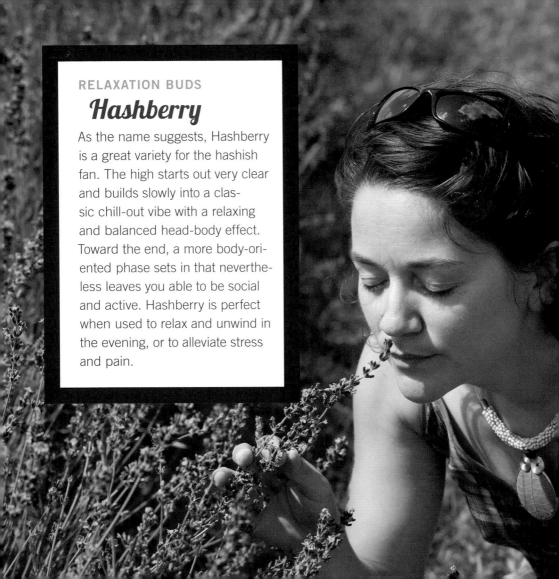

RELAXATION BUDS
Hashberry

As the name suggests, Hashberry is a great variety for the hashish fan. The high starts out very clear and builds slowly into a classic chill-out vibe with a relaxing and balanced head-body effect. Toward the end, a more body-oriented phase sets in that nevertheless leaves you able to be social and active. Hashberry is perfect when used to relax and unwind in the evening, or to alleviate stress and pain.

How to Make a Lavender Sachet

Feeling stressed? Explore other plants for your aroma and herbal therapy. Lavender—besides smelling great—alleviates muscle pain, headaches and stress. Place fresh lavender in your surroundings to feel more contentment. Use dried flowers to make a lavender sachet (pouch) for long-lasting relief. Place the sachet under your pillow for sweet dreams.

Materials

1/3 cup dried lavender flowers (stems removed)

Hemp or cotton muslin fabric

Narrow ribbon

Scissors

Method

Cut fabric in a 10" square or circle. Place lavender flowers in a pile in the center of the fabric.

Bunch the fabric around the lavender and tie a ribbon around the top. You can add elastic before the ribbon to keep it secure.

Kandahar

This variety captures the complexity of a street bazaar with sour-sweet fragrances. The high settles deep in the body with a potential for couchlock. Down-tempo music, television, or other undemanding yet sensory activities pair well with Kandahar's sedating qualities. It's all good—sit back, soak it in and enjoy the satisfying sense of relaxation.

Northern Lights

Northern Lights is one of the most potent and well-known indica varieties; in fact, its name has become synonymous with "marijuana" for even nonusers of cannabis. The aroma is pungently sweet and the taste is a flavorful mixture of sweet and spicy. The high is more of a potent physical experience than feels comfortably lazy and relaxing.

Blues Busting

We all have off days, when blue skies turn to grey and the outlook reads grim. Getting out of bed can seem like an insurmountable task when the Sad Clown is running the show. Unless you shove an upbeat, euphoria-inducing spliff into his droopy mouth, that's it! Head toward the light and embrace the small pleasures that bring us joy—like a white, fluffy ash and a light, breezy attitude. Whether it's a shift into quiet bliss, the courage to wildly abandon inhibitions or the motivation to make a positive change, these strains are all truly happy buds.

Tip:

Cinco de Mayo often falls around the same time as the Global Marijuana March. Celebrate both by having a Mexican-themed marijuana party. Put on a sombrero, make THC-infused tacos, blast the mariachi music and get blasted on strains from south of the border (like Colombian Gold). Fill a piñata with papers, filters, packs of screens, and even joints. Then grab a blindfold, and you've got yourself a smokin' fiesta. Olé!

*"Hurry, get on, now it's coming,
Listen to those rails a-humming"
—"Take the A-Train,"
Duke Ellington & Charles Mingus*

BLISSFUL BUDS

A-Train

On the menthol-lemon inhale, A-Train brings you a satisfying, well-balanced mind and body lift for a clear and productive high. The exhale numbs the lips with bits of sweet Afghan hashiness. A-Train brings you home; you can drop your baggage from the day. This strain's creeper high gradually slows you down a notch or two, but it won't stun you into a stupor. It's a combination of two strains—Arcata Trainwreck and Mazar-i-Sharif Afghan—It is widely used medically for alleviating mind and body discomfort.

Mekong High

Mekong High is an original, fresh, pure-smoking sativa that reminds people of the way sativas used to be. The buds are sticky and scented with an intoxicating, spicy aroma. The taste is distinctively earthy and pleasant. The true highlight of this strain is its happy, uplifting effect. It is exceptionally clear, making it wonderful for creative pursuits and socializing.

Blue Buddha

The Blue Buddha flavor is velvety deep, with a dank skunkiness and a slightly sweet, blueberry creaminess. At first it lifts you up then it wraps you in a blanket of fogginess. The first wave is a spurt of energy that shifts into a moderately long-lasting couchlock. Blue Buddha enhances the contemplative mood, indulging the imagination, reflection and artistic impulses.

Tip:

Go on a date...with yourself. Check out stoner events in your area that you're curious about but never have time to do. They don't need to be overtly marijuana-themed to attract the stoner kind: live music, poetry readings and art exhibits attract the like-minded. Activist events like rallies and festivals are another great way to boost good karma and meet new friends, all the while fighting prohibition.

Marijuana Masala Chai

What happens when you mix a traditionally sweet, spicy and steaming pick-me-up with another, just-as-traditional Indian indulgence? According to Ayurvedic philosophy, chai is mood-lifting, calming and revitalizing—the perfect cup of cheer to reward oneself.

Ingredients

1 cup of your favorite chai tea bag

2 tsp cannabis milk

1 tsp sugar

Instructions

Mix cannabis milk and sugar in with a cup of hot tea.

** Recipe from *Aunt Sandy's Medical Marijuana Cookbook: Comfort Food for Body and Mind* by Sandy Moriarty

Cannabis Milk Recipe

Ingredients

1/8 oz cannabis buds

2 cups milk, cream or soymilk

Instructions

Over low heat, mix together buds and milk. Bring to a rolling boil. Reduce heat and simmer for 30 minutes. Cool and strain the plant material from the milk.

**Cannabis Milk recipe from *Aunt Sandy's Medical Marijuana Cookbook: Comfort Food for Body and Mind* by Sandy Moriarty.

Tip:

Take toke breaks outside in the sunshine. Or, if you live in a particularly cloudy/inhospitable environment, toke in front of a special light that will boost your vitamin D levels and your mood. These lights are found online and are relatively inexpensive. They are used to treat seasonal affective disorder (SAD). Using SAD lights or taking vitamin D supplements help maintain strong bones and contribute to a healthy, happy frame of mind.

Sour Diesel IBL

Sour Diesel's high is a soaring, psychedelic, lemon-flavored lift into the sunshine. It levels out in a clear-headed euphoria, good for most activities aside from operating heavy machinery and driving that golf cart too fast. Overindulging can limit activities to the recreational, but moderate toking puts you in a deeply good mood. It is a great stone for letting go of negativity. Many medicinal users find Sour Diesel a good variety for treating sadness and pain.

2005 *High Times* Strain of the Year award

The Purps

The buds are tasty looking and smelling, with deep purple coloring and a frosting of resin. The flavors are soothing and tantalizing, lingering pleasurably on the tongue. The Purps high soars into a long-lasting purple haze of playful euphoria. It produces an active awake feeling with a very low burnout factor. A nice antidote to depression, these rich flavored buds turn the blues to the purps.

Carnival

True to her name, Carnival is vibrant with fresh and enticing flavor elements that range from sugary dry grape to lemon and haze. It enters the senses quickly creating a lucid and humorous merrymaking mood. Celebrate life and forget about the workaday world for a while.

Tip:

When you're down in the dumps, get rid of stress with fitness. Yoga, qi gong and tai chi relax the mind, center and strengthen the body, and help with flexibility. But don't get so stoned that you lose balance. It's not very serene when you take down half the yoga class when you're pin-wheeling your arms into a fall and hit the ground.

Wappa

Wappa's fruity nugs are great head candy. The buzz comes on strong, but with a pleasant, rather than jarring, onset. It's a luminous high that nudges open the doors of perception. After a few hours, the heightened awareness fades off slowly. Even though she is a full indica, Wappa does not weigh down the body or create couchlock. She taps into an active, aware body vibe, more conducive to merrymaking than couch surfing.

Mako Haze

Mako Haze smoke is lovely and smooth, with a heavy hazy taste and her high is up, up, up! Haze strains like the Mako are good treatments for lethargy and depression. Mako Haze has a therapeutic effect on the mental state of anyone who appreciates a quality high.

1st Place Sativa 2006 *High Times* Cannabis Cup

Apollo 13BX

Apollo 13BX is the type of strain that earns marijuana nicknames like "the fruit." These lime-green buds have a heavy, dank smell of overripe fruit, a mixture of rich sultry mangoes, acidic lemons and an underlying pepper tickle that comes through in the aftertaste. This is a motivational strain. With just a few hits, many people are inspired to get stuff done, whether writing, cleaning, working in the yard, taking photos, or going on a hike in the great outdoors. It is an up, happy-yet-purposeful high that invigorates as well as a cup of good coffee.

"See that look in their eyes?
You gotta get that look back, Rock.
Eye of the tiger, man."
—Apollo Creed in *Rocky III*

HAPPY BUDS

Herbal Meditations

The inner journey can be the most treacherous, but with the mind's balm in the form of dank strains of cannabis, the way will be well-lit and smooth as silk. Create the destinies you envision by centering your thoughts, being mindful of your surroundings and finding inspiration in the minutiae of life. You can choose to take in the entire garden, your vision filled with a sea of green—or concentrate on a single trichome on a single calyx on a single bud on a single plant.

Tip:

Deep breathing and awareness of breath are the keys to quieting your mind. Vaporize just prior to meditating, rather than smoking, to give your lungs a break and to keep you from being distracted by coughing fits. If you have sensitive lungs, avoid burning incense and try a candle or oil diffuser instead. Some vaporizers come with an attachment to diffuse essential oils while you're vaporizing your weed, creating a beautiful scent décor of your choosing in your environment.

The Church

The Church grants mental stimulation and ease, followed by a steady descent into the body, which feels clean and tranquil. Hints of spring flowers and red berries keep the flavor light and sweet. Rather than heavy-hitting, The Church offers a mild, focused, balancing, progressive high.

Visions of Mother Ganja

In Hindu and Buddhist traditions a mandala is a geometric symbol meant to represent the universe. Meditating on the meaning and symbolism of a mandala and how it pertains to your own life can be a centering experience in your quest for completeness and self-unity. Look at the mandala as a whole, or concentrate on a small aspect of it; either way, it may strike a chord in your psyche.

CENTERING BUDS

Fruit of the Gods (FOG)

FOG tastes sweet with a hazy, floral perfume that lingers throughout the room in a thick, white cloud. The FOG high is clearheaded and uplifting. It's very functional and easy to maintain and is excellent for both work and socializing. The buzz creates a momentum to get things done and motivate with friends, or focus on a project.

CENTERING BUDS

Orange Bud

Orange Bud leaves a citrus note on the tongue, with hints of sweetness like a very ripe orange or tangerine. By the time the taste registers on the tongue, the buzz is palpable. Orange Bud is an uplifting, active mental stone, compatible with any activity. Its fast onset makes it attractive for medical relief from nausea and obsessive, distracting thoughts.

Hawaiian Snow

Hawaiian Snow's rich spicy sativa taste refreshes with mint on exhale. Its complex aroma evokes eucalyptus, lemon grass and a hint of musk and green moss. It is a lovely social high that lowers tensions and incites laughter.

Kushage

You may need to re-examine your concepts time to time. This strain's sativa-dominant high is a great mind opener for brainstorms, conceptualizing, or creating artwork. It is less favorable when efficiency or punctuality are on the agenda.

3rd place sativa award, 2005 *High Times* Cannabis Cup

Tip:

Try to make meditation a daily practice by setting aside the same time each day. If you can faithfully observe 4:20 daily, you can commit to taking as long as it would take to smoke a joint, a couple of times a day, to improve your mind and expand your consciousness.

MINDFUL BUDS
Somantra

Somantra buds are very hard and thickly carpeted with THC crystals. The dominant flavor is reminiscent of a ripe mango mixed with some good cheese. Like its namesake, Somantra awakens a sense of cosmic clarity. The effects let one soar into the wondrous mystery of existence, inspiring thoughtful time spent with friends and a great appreciation of melody and art.

Create a Manifestation Board

Materials

*Bulletin board, poster board,
   or framed area on a wall*

*Old magazines, photos, symbols,
   and other inspirational images*

Instructions

Think about your goals and
aspirations. Use an image to
represent your idea of what
you want in your life and pin it to
your bulletin board. The images
should help create inspiration
for the changes you want to see.

Example: If you want a new
bong, include an image of the
bong you want. If you want your
dealer to get better weed, scan
and put up pics of the stash
you desire.

INSPIRATIONAL BUDS

Flo

Flo has an energetic, motivating buzz with unusual clarity. This is true wake 'n' bake pot, great to start the day off right without losing site of your intentions. The flavor has a floral quality similar to Napalese Temple Hash, with a touch of blueberry tones. The smell echoes the taste, remaining subtle and light.

1st Place 2000 *Cannabis Culture* **Cup**

"The original Flo has always been a personal favorite of mine. Flo's fruity-floral bouquet and taste make me feel all giggly-girly and it gets my creative juices flowing"
–Mamakind, author of SexPot: The Marijuana Lover's Guide to Gettin' It On

INSPIRATIONAL BUDS
Nirvana Special

Nirvana Special's high dissolves apathy and laziness. It's energetic, blissful, and playful. This variety can enhance an afternoon of barbecue and Frisbee, or a morning of creative work. Connoisseurs who make cannabis part of an active life will appreciate this strain's taste and buzz.

Blueberry Haze

This hybrid inherits the taste that goes with the name: a succulent berry flavor with a bit of the fresh herbal hue of the Haze. The true reward is the quality of the high, which builds from a mild feeling of wellness to euphoria, inspiration and perma-grin. The potency and gradual onset require some experience and pacing; overuse may turn an enjoyable buzz into sweet dreams, as overwhelming drowsiness kicks in.

Wake 'n' Bake

Whether your day starts at the crack of dawn, or you don't roll out of bed until evening sets in, the first toke of the day is the most important. Your initial stone sets the tone for everything that comes after and if you're not much of a morning person, you need all the help you can get to start the day off right. A hearty breakfast, a cuppa joe, the morning paper/Facebook check-in and a hit from the bong will send you on your way with a song in your heart and a spring in your step, ready to tackle whatever life has in store.

Tip:

You know how your mom always bugged you to lay out your clothes for the next day, the night before? She was right—if by "clothes," she really meant "weed." There's nothing worse than being hung over or just plain tired and you can't find your papers. Then you can't find your lighter. Then you can't find your stash and then you're late and you haven't even gotten dressed and so on…. Why not make your mornings a little more sane by making sure, before you go to bed, that everything's together in one easily accessible place—the same place, every time.

CAFFEINATED BUDS
Buddha Haze

This is one of the sweeter tasting hazes out there, mixing pungent, sweet fruit flavors with a mango edge and a hint of bubblegum. The Buddha Haze high has no ceiling—the sky is the limit. The strong and seamless beginning builds in a long euphoric rush, making Buddha Haze good for parties and festivities of all kinds. The buzz is very functional, because it creates an alert, electric and cheerful vibe that inspires thought, without causing one's mind to wander off.

The Iced Ask Ed-puccino

Grab a spliff of the good stuff and a cup modelled after the Guru of Ganja's personal morning brew. You and Ed Rosenthal can't help but be bright-eyed and bushy tailed enough to take on just about anything—even thirty-odd years of questions about cannabis cultivation—with the best of them.

1. Prepare regular brewed coffee

2. Pour the coffee into a tall mug or glass, about ¾ full

3. Add one or two teaspoons of sugar

4. Add three ice cubes

5. Top off with chocolate soymilk

6. Stir well and enjoy

Kaya

Kaya has a spicy flavor refreshingly different from other strains, pairing well with a latte or London Fog. She has a sweet kiss that lingers on the tongue. The high is also different from the punch-out associated with some popular "skunk" strains—a return to the mellower potencies of days gone by. Kaya is unlikely to waylay lightweight smokers on the first bong hit and she is a great daytime friend to those who prefer a high that is more like a "snack" than a "meal," or desire a stone that is easier to moderate.

CAFFEINATED BUDS

White Russian

An expansive smoke, White Russian has a clear high with a long duration. The effect can be complex, but tends toward wakefulness rather than sleep and may have some trippy or spacey dimensions. A good 4:20 smoke with a cup of coffee, when you're ready to kick back and relax.

Tip:

Set up a lifetime of happy mornings. Greeting the day with a Sensi & Sunrise Salutation can freshen the mind and body. This will ensure clarity and focus throughout the rest of your day and into the night.

Step 1. Joint Mountain Pose—Stand with your feet together. Bring hands palm to palm in front of your heart.

Step 2. Gandalf Pipe Pose—Raise arms and stretch over head, lean slightly backwards. Do not strain or over-stretch.

Step 3. Folding Bowl Pose—While exhaling, slowly bend forward toward toes and place palms to the ground.

Step 4. Dropped Baggie Pose—Move into a deep forward lunge by extending right leg behind you. Keep head up and both hands on the ground for stability.

Step 5. Rolling Board Pose—Extend both legs behind you into the plank pose.

Step 6. Chillum Pose—Lower body onto arms as if doing a push-up, hold pose for a breath then transition into filter rolling pose.

Step 7. Filter Rolling Pose—From the push-up position, lower pelvis into ground, lift head upwards, and lean head backwards.

Step 8. Creasing the Paper Pose—Shift weight forward onto arms, raise your hips. You should be facing down, eye-level to knees.

Step 9. Dropped Lighter Pose—Extend left leg back into a deep forward lunge. Keep head up and both hands on the ground.

Step 10. Roach Pose—Keeping hands on ground, bring feet together, exhale while standing up into a forward bend.

Step 11. Vapor Bag Pose—Slowly rise, stretching hands over head, then slightly lean back.

Step 12. Sparking Another Pose— Stand with your feet together. Bring hands palm to palm at the heart.

Morning Star

Morning Star produces a cheerful, upbeat and functional buzz, which makes it a great smoke among friends. The high comes on quickly and is fairly long lasting. This is a great smoke to start off the day. With its delightful taste and motivational high, it may become your Morning Star. The taste has a fruity lemon-citrus subtlety, even exuding a slight citrus tone on the exhale, reminiscent of Earl Grey tea.

"The bright morning star, day's harbinger."
—John Milton

Strawberry Cough

Strawberry Cough tickles the lungs with a creamy-sweet smoke, whose flavor resembles strawberry, perhaps with a kiwi fruit complement. The buzz is heady and active, a classic let's-go-hiking sativa lift that can alleviate depression.

Sativa Spirit

Sativa Spirit is a pleasure to smoke. With a taste like dark berries or red grapes, this strain has a smooth inhale and the energetic buzz comes on fast. Users crave human interaction—like a trip to the beach or a nightclub, rather than staying locked to the couch and glued to the tube. This high also motivates adults to finish their chores—routine, non-hazardous tasks like cleaning, filing and gardening. It's a happy high that can lighten the mood and spark creativity.

Tip:

Sativa hybrid dominant strains are famous for inducing appetite. If a bowl of wake 'n' bake doesn't get your stomach grumbling, try cooking. Even if you're not hungry, the sight and scents should stimulate your senses and get those taste buds watering.

BREAKFAST BUDS

Critical #47

The Critical #47 buzz is calm, with lucid sativa influences and a touch of munchie-inducement. In terms of taste, this variety is a skillful blend of two sweet varieties—Critical Mass and AK47—that deliver a fruity mango-peach flavor infused with vanilla overtones. This strain is perfect to partake in before digging into a buttery, syrupy stack of waffles or pancakes.

Raspberry Cough

The high from these frosty colas is awake, yet tranquil. It has a clear-headed, alert and functional, yet peaceful, influence. It is also rejuvenating for the spirit and serves as a great companion for healthy activities such as nature hikes, meditation, or savoring the vibrant flavors of the best food nature has to offer. Raspberry Cough's smoke has an expansive quality. It is a profusion of herb, mint, spice and tropical-floral freshness.

Whitaker Blues

Whitaker Blues has a complex and enchanting scent that ranges from pungent to sweet. One may get hints of a floral berry candy with a distinct velvety grape flavor. This variety mixes the high, beginning with a strong stimulation that increases inspiration, sensuality and appetite. The perfect accompaniment to breakfast in bed.

Working It

We gotta pay the bills and keep the taxman at bay—hopefully with a little something left over to pick up a gram or two of sweet salvation. We should all be so lucky, making a living doing something we truly enjoy and believe in. Unfortunately this often isn't the case, so it's helpful to have a coffee-break treat that makes the 9-to-5 rat race move along at a slightly swifter pace. Even the most mundane of chores can be made at least tolerable if you invite the Mary Poppins of the plant world in to provide that bowl-full of sugar to help the medicine go down.

Tip:

Be a smart stoner. If your job involves safety issues for you and/or others, wait until your days off to partake and never, ever show up to work high, no matter how well you think you can control your stone. Not only is it dangerous, you'll give all potheads a bad name and we'll never be able to get it legalized. It will be entirely your fault.

Tip:

Medicated eye drops are sometimes essential for taking away the telltale red eyes that belie your toking up. However, overuse of these drops can actually cause reddening, so use them sparingly. While marijuana is a vasodilator that contributes to red eyes, often the culprit is eye dryness, so try plain saline first. That's far gentler to your peepers.

Tip:

If you're lucky enough to be able to have your vaporizer at work with you at your desk, choose a whip-style machine, rather than one that blows air into a bag. Not only are there fewer parts to deal with, but the blowing of the fan used to fill the bag and the crinkling of the bag itself can be disturbing to others and give your activities away when you're on a long conference call.

INTELLECTUAL BUDS
Thai-Tanic

Cannabis aficionados love Thai varieties. "Thai sticks" imparted a light citrus taste, with an edge of tang and a chocolate chaser, to the mouths of veteran pot connoisseurs. Thai-Tanic recaptures those sweet-scented memories. The buzz arrives quickly, delivering a vivid trippiness, stoking the mental furnace. Eventually this levels out to a dreamy attitude, as new concepts drift and play in your mind.

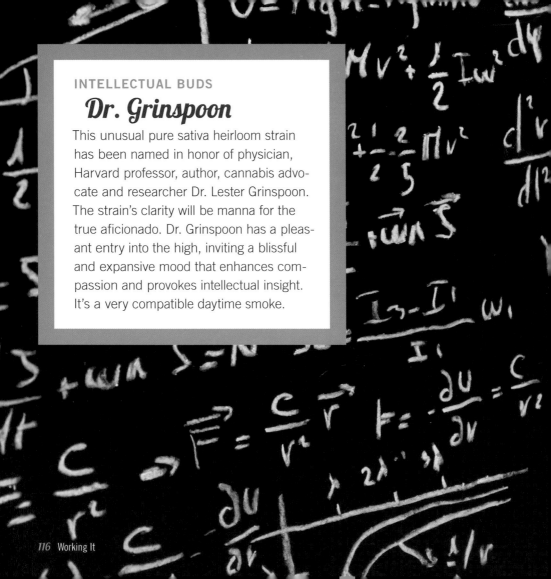

Dr. Grinspoon

This unusual pure sativa heirloom strain has been named in honor of physician, Harvard professor, author, cannabis advocate and researcher Dr. Lester Grinspoon. The strain's clarity will be manna for the true aficionado. Dr. Grinspoon has a pleasant entry into the high, inviting a blissful and expansive mood that enhances compassion and provokes intellectual insight. It's a very compatible daytime smoke.

INTELLECTUAL BUDS
White Satin

This robust variety is subtle in aroma and silky smooth in taste. The buds exude a mild apricot fragrance and fresh, sweet taste. White Satin is a pleasure smoke, with a fresh, mentally stimulating high and no heavy body or mind incapacitation. That makes this variety the thinker's very functional choice for daytime enjoyment.

Shoe-Hash

If your job requires you to be on your feet all day, why not get more out of it than just a lousy paycheck? Heat and pressure are what turn good kief into fine hashish, so if you're lucky enough to find yourself with some, use this technique and thank your poor tired feet, because they'll give you a mighty fine reward at the end of a long, hard work day.

Place one to three grams (about a tablespoon) of keif in a pile in the middle of a 6" x 6" square of plastic wrap. You can fold it up into a small square of parchment paper first. This prevents the keif from sticking to the plastic wrap. Fold up the kief/parchment paper package into the larger plastic wrap square. You should now have a small square package approximately 2" x 2". Use a piece of duct tape wrapped around the entire package to seal it. Slip it into the heel of your shoe. You might notice it at first, but it shouldn't be too big that it bothers you too much. The more weight you put on it, the hotter your feet get and the more you move around, the better the result. At the end of the day, carefully cut open your package(s) and you'll find a beautifully worked piece of hash, to smoke away those sore muscles.

Big Buddha Cheese

Taste is where this variety shines. The flavor has a special "dank" quality reminiscent of what good pot used to taste like—spicy, sweet and kush-like. The high is very up. It can be consumed every day with little to no immunity, nor change in quality of the high, making BBC suitable to those who need to get things done sooner than later

Northern Lights x Haze

NL-Haze delivers fresh, spicy, sativa-type buds that have a clean, peppery taste. An immediate cerebral high, this pot has sometimes been referred to as "speed weed" in Holland. Overall, NL-Haze has a friendly high with a trippy edge that adds some extra zing to any day, lightening even the heaviest of loads.

Kali Mist

With a scent and flavor that spans both the sweet and spicy, this cerebral high leaves the mind clear and focused. Kali Mist's effects have proven beneficial for medical users with MS, fatigue and chronic pain. Kali Mist is a great all-day pot that can enhance energetic physical activities.

Headband

The Headband is like a reassuring brain hug and its presence brings a heightened awareness of your gray matter. Imagine a strain that when smoked, mimics that feeling; moving rapidly from the front of the mind to the back, easing anxiety while inducing awareness. The high is not too overpowering and lasts a long time. It's a good utility daytime smoke. Its uniquely enjoyable fuel-sour taste makes it a memorable smoke that makes time fly by.

"Wrapped right around my melon, you're a product like Magellan."
- "Headband," cast of Glee

Euforia

This sweet, blossom-scented variety delivers a very pleasing and up high. It is an active pot, useful medicinally when marijuana's soothing properties need to be balanced with lucidity and energy. Euforia adds smiles to the recreational smoker's day, without hampering other activities, when used in moderation.

REPETITIVE CHORE BUDS

Ice

Ice practically fumes with the nearly fuel-like scent of raw THC. Flavored like Nepali black hash, toking Ice is likely to induce coughing, so keep the water bottle handy. Plan on putting your brain on ice and letting your body take over, switching you into autopilot.

1st Place 1998 *High Times* Cannabis Cup

Hittin' the Sack

It's been said that we spend around one-third of our lifetime in bed. It's a good thing that there are so many wonderful things to do in a horizontal position other than just sleeping (though sleeping is definitely high on the list). We need sleep to recharge our batteries; to heal the wounds the day has inflicted upon us and indeed, perchance to dream. Perhaps to dream about what we'd do—and with whom we'd do it—in our beds during our waking hours. The best method of invoking Nyx and Aphrodite—the goddesses of sleep and love—is to burn a sacrament of cannabis and let your world-weariness go up in a puff of smoke.

Tip:

Pick up a tray for serving breakfast in bed and turn it into a stable, portable toking station. Stock it with all of your bedtime must-haves—pipe or papers, grinder, small ashtray, lighter, favorite pot-related books and magazines, etc.

"To be in love is merely to be in a state of perceptual anesthesia—to mistake an ordinary young woman for a goddess."
-H.L. Mencken

POWER NAP BUDS

Anesthesia

Anesthesia is named for the narcotic body stone that its smoke induces. This variety causes a deep physical mellowing that slowly works through one's limbs like a warm blanket, while allowing the mind to stay engaged. As a medicinal-strength strain, it may be too potent to be enjoyable for beginners or casual recreational smokers. However, patients who rely on indica body effects, but want to stay mentally alert will enjoy the balance of these qualities. The old school taste is earthy and dark, with a hint of coffee tones that will appeal to fans of rich hashy flavors.

POWER NAP BUDS
Soma A+

The indica buzz is relaxing to the body and mind, which is good for quiet contemplation or snoozing on rainy day afternoons. Better as a day-ender than a day-starter, Soma A+ provides medicinal-quality cannabis with healing properties for what ails you, whether physical, psychological, or spiritual in nature.

Vanilla Kush

Kushes are known for their high THC levels and this variety delivers a potent and long-lasting high that's particularly strong in its physical effects. Vanilla Kush is also standout in taste. The strong, sweet, herbal-floral notes dominate the smoke. This variety induces a strong sense of relaxation, easing muscle tension. In smaller amounts, the mental effects are euphoric and thoughtful, yet relaxed. Heavy indulgence strengthens these effects, leading to a trippy and potentially sleepy tunnel vision that may induce couchlock or napping.

2nd Place 2009 *High Times* Cannabis Cup

Tip:

Cannabis isn't the only natural remedy to help you catch forty winks. Make sure you check with a pharmacist if you're taking other medications—natural or otherwise—and conditions that might interfere with the action of these substances or vice versa. Try these pharmaceutical-free suggestions for inviting the Sandman in:

Melatonin

Valerian

Hops

Catnip/Catmint

Chamomile

Passion Flower

Kava

5-HTP

Lavender

Clary Sage

Lemon Balm

Herijuana

Herijuana (rhymes with marijuana), when smoked reveals itself quickly in an intense, deeply physical and long-lasting sedative stone. This is not a buzz for the lighthearted. The smell is hashy and incense-like; the taste is smooth with light sandalwood and dark coffee essences.

DEEP SLEEP BUDS

Querkle

Querkle is mostly a nightcap smoke and may encourage late-night snacking, if you can stay awake. The buzz comes on slowly and lasts a long time. The strain's primo taste and gradual buzz may take discipline to avoid the heavy zoned stone of overindulgence.

Cataract Kush

The Cataract is so named because it brings on the squinty-eyed, Mr. Magoo stone that penetrates deep into the body. Combine that with a creeper effect and it can cause serious couchlock for the un-initiated. Those who are after the big body stone indica will be pleased with the hashy, spicy-sweet flavor that brings the rich pungency of Eastern spices. Medical users will enjoy this strain's usefulness for pain relief, encouragement of appetite and assistance with sleep.

𝒜 Toker's 𝐹oreplay

Take turns pleasing each other. As the joint gets going, so do you. Start seducing your partner. As they puff-puff, you fluff-fluff. Switch places when the joint is passed. By the time your spliff is finished, the two of you will just be getting started.

CannaSutra

CannaSutra's mild yet mood-elevating high boosts mental focus, rather than derailing it, making this a good all-day or all-night smoke. It's particularly appropriate for those who like to toke when they sit down for a session of computer or graphic work, or for getting philosophical with friends. The strain's name—from the Sanskrit love manual *Kama Sutra*—also suggests profound exhilarations between lovers, opening the chakras in tantric ecstasy. The smoke is incense-like, sweet, aromatic and soft.

Tip:

Try a hemp-based lube next time you find yourself in a tight 'n' sticky situation in the boudoir. They're made from plant-based materials and don't have condom-eating oil-based products in them. They are also water-soluble and therefore, easy to clean up.

GETTIN' IT ON BUDS
Passion Queen

Passion Queen's fast high rises steadily for the first hour, then levels out to a stratospheric cruising orbit for three to four hours of knowing grins and deep, pleasant thoughts. This is a good smoke for cheering up and having fun with a passionate partner. The mind and body soar in perfect union, as do the tokers themselves.

Strawberry Haze

Aside from the expected, very sugary strawberry aroma (which is much sweeter than most sativas), the scent has been compared to summer blossoms, rose petals and red berries. Her high is fast hitting, clear, creative and giggly. It's good for social moments, as well as for introspective ones. Chasing the blues away, making love, making friends laugh and making art are all recommended activities to accompany this strain (especially if you can do all four at once).

The Holidaze

The holidays—no matter which holidays they are—are the most joyous and stressful times in our lives. Good cheer and merrymaking can sometimes turn into angst and subsequently, boredom. This is when the gift of ganja really comes into play, for all three eventualities. Undo your belt and hit the couch after the turkey and candied yams are cleared away, to enjoy a puff worthy of Old Saint Nick himself (surely he's not flying around the world and eating all those milk and cookies in one night with anything but the dank in his pipe). Or maybe you're celebrating the miracle of miracles: can you make one night's worth of oil last eight? If it's honey oil, you'll certainly try.

Tip:

Passing on the booze and instead, sticking to the herb, could save you from gaining extra holiday pounds that high-calorie alcoholic drinks harbor. Bud might save you from slipping into the depression that sometimes accompanies certain times of the year, save you from the things you might say to that family member you hate and save you from losing your job, because you took one too many photocopies of your bare ass during the office party.

Budderscotch Sauce

This sweet, creamy and oh-so-pot-dreamy sauce is the perfect accompaniment for any holiday desert (or even over the Sunday brunch pancakes).

Ingredients

1 cup sugar

¼ cup light corn syrup

3 tbsp water

¼ cup unsalted cannabutter

1 tsp cider vinegar

½ cup heavy cream

2 tsp vanilla

Pinch of salt

Instructions

In a heavy saucepan bring sugar, corn syrup and water to a boil over moderate heat, stirring until sugar is dissolved. Boil mixture (without stirring, but occasionally swirling mixture around in the pan) until a golden caramel color is reached. Remove pan from heat and add cannabutter, vinegar and a pinch of salt, swirling (not stirring) contents until cannabutter is melted. Add cream and vanilla and simmer, stirring, for one minute (sauce will be a golden brown color). Cool sauce to room temperature. It will thicken as it cools. Pour into lidded jars and keep in the fridge (keeps for about three weeks) and serve either warmed up or at room temperature.

DESSERT BUDS

Lemon Skunk

Lemon Skunk is a tasty sweet citrus bud for those who like fresh fruity stash. The enjoyable sativa-leaning high boosts the senses, bringing on thoughtful reflection and heightened sensory perception. It may also boost the sense for a need to go spelunk through the fridge for some serious snacking.

1st Place 2009 *High Times*
  Top 10 Strains of the Year
1st Place 2008 Spannabis Cup
1st Place 2007 Highlife Cup

Millennium

Millennium has a heavy, hashy bouquet, but the flavor is earthy and sweet with sandalwood tones. This is not pot to smoke on your way into work or when you're going to need to drive anywhere soon. Millennium offers a strongly physical, intense buzz for some couch potato time in front of the fire. The pantry may also be subject to raiding when the munchies take hold.

DESSERT BUDS
Tahoe Gold

Tahoe Gold invites a relaxing state of body and mind. Its functional buzz gradually takes effect, like sailing over a gentle breeze. It invites a playful and positive attitude. The scent and flavors are tropical and sweet, like pungent berry candy. Medical patients with chronic pain conditions may find this strain offers effective pain relief in combination with a lucid and awake state of mind and a happy attitude. Tahoe Gold is the perfect punctuation to a sumptuous meal.

Tip:

Spinning a dreidel isn't only for kids. It's a gambling game (you can find easy instructions online) and if you switch playing for the traditional coins and nuts for buds and chunks of hash, you've got yourself a gelt-free good time at your next adult Hanukkah get-together. Pass the pot-ato pancakes, please!

The OG #18

The high feels like a bubble stretched around you. When the bubble pops, it's as if the high caused time to warp. The clock doesn't seem to match the personal perception of time. These qualities make The OG #18 optimal for focused leisure such as playing video games, but a terrible idea for driving or staying on schedule.

GAMING BUDS

Veryberry (remix)

Cured buds sing with fruity, sweet and fresh berry aromas. This pleasantly awake, happy and energetic sensation builds up gradually into a soaring yet functional state of bliss. It's good for fun with friends, in the sunny outdoors or at home playing video games and chilling.

GAMING BUDS
Southern Nights

Southern Nights's high is a positive mind-body effect that's great any time of day. It encourages activities that stimulate the senses in a hands-on way. This may involve acting on a creative impulse, going for a hike, gaming, or indulging in other sensual appetites.

Tip:

Need a breather? Family gathering driving you nutbar? Try some of these tried, tested and true excuses to take the four-twenty needed to sneak-a-toke:

Booze/mixer/ice run. Don't forget to come back with something other than smelly fingers

Fresh air. Mixed with smoke, sure, but fresh nonetheless

Important phone call to take outside. Might as well keep up appearances by at least giving your dealer a call

Check out the neighborhood. If you take a brisk walk, you'll be gone before passersbys notice the scent of your revelry

Visit an old friend, old lover, or favorite spot. Better yet, your favorite spot where you used to go with old friends and lovers to get ripped

DRAMA DIMINISHING BUDS
Skunk Haze

The Skunk Haze is a straightforward combo of two classic strains. It's primarily a head buzz with a lingering body stone that carries through. Overall, this variety has an energetic and clearheaded, yet leisurely, effect that reduces anxiety and lowers the paranoia quotient.

DRAMA DIMINISHING BUDS
Fruity Thai

The most notable features of this variety are her scent and flavor. Fruity Thai releases a fresh fruity aroma. The taste has overtones of lemon and lime. The effect is a comfortable, dreamy, but functional high. The vibe is sensual and communicative, happy and playful and lightens a heavy mood.

Swiss Cheese

Swiss Cheese buds are dark and hard with a twist on typical skunk aromas. The mix of earthy skunk pungency, with old school musk and a hint of candy, has an edge that makes it unique. This is an eighteen-wheeler type of buzz; a heavy, fast-onset stone that may not be sedative, but will definitely slow things down and give smokers a stereotypical eye-droop. Most people will probably lose the urge to exert much energy after smoking this strain and be content to watch sports or movies, or engage in some other undemanding pastime, but some might crave mellower, open-ended recreation, like the desire to take a leisurely hike or even a jog or just get some air.

Activities Index by Variety

Seed Companies and Varieties

APOTHECARY
Grandaddy Grape Ape

USA
www.apothecarygenetics.com
info@apothecarygenetics.com

BARNEY'S FARM
Dr. Grinspoon
LSD
Vanilla Kush

The Netherlands
www.barneys.biz

BC BUD DEPOT
Blue Buddha
The Purps

Canada
www.bcbuddepot.com

BIG BUDDHA SEEDS
Big Buddha Cheese
Buddha Haze
Chiesel

United Kingdom
www.bigbuddhaseeds.com

CERES SEEDS
Fruity Thai
Skunk Haze

The Netherlands
www.ceresseeds.com
info@ceresseeds.com

DELTA-9 LABS
CannaSutra
Fruit of the Gods (FOG)

The Netherlands
www.delta9labs.com
info@delta9labs.com

DJ SHORT
Blueberry
Flo
Vanilluna
Whitaker Blues

USA/Canada
www.greatcanadianseeds.com
www.legendseeds.com

DNA GENETICS/ RESERVA PRIVADA
Blueberry Haze
Cataract Kush
Headband
Lemon Skunk
The OG#18

The Netherlands
www.dnagenetics.com
info@dnagenetics.com

DUTCH PASSION

Euforia

Mekong High

Orange Bud

PolarLight

Strawberry Cough

The Netherlands
www.dutchpassion.nl

FAST SEED BANK

Southern Nights

Spain
www.fastseedbank.com
info@fastseedbank.com

FLYING DUTCHMEN

Pineapple Punch

Thai-Tanic

Titan's Haze

The Netherlands
www.flyingdutchmen.com
info@flyingdutchmen.com

GREEN HOUSE SEED CO

AMS

Arjan's Ultra Haze #2

Hawaiian Snow

Strawberry Haze

Super Lemon Haze

The Church

The Netherlands
www.greenhouseseeds.nl
www.kingofcannabis.com
orders@greenhouse.org

GREENTHUMB SEEDS

Millennium

Canada
www.drgreenthumb.com
drgreenthumb@drgreenthumb.com

HEAD SEEDS
Represented by:
Gypsy Nirvana's
Seed Boutique

Casey Jones

G-13 Diesel

United Kingdom
www.seedboutique.com
orders@seedboutique.com

HUMBOLDT SEED
ORGANISATION

Veryberry (remix)

United Kingdom
www.humboldtseeds.co.uk
info@humboldtseeds.co.uk

KIWISEEDS

Mako Haze

Kiwiskunk

The Netherlands
www.kiwiseeds.com
info@kiwiseeds.com

MANDALA SEEDS

Hashberry

Mandala #1

Satori

Speed Queen

White Satin

Spain
www.mandalaseeds.com
info@mandalaseeds.com

MASTER THAI ORGANICS
Tahoe Gold

USA
www.masterthai.com
master_thaigardens@yahoo.com

MINISTRY OF CANNABIS
Carnival
Kandahar

The Netherlands
www.ministryofcannabis.com
info@ministryofcannabis.com

NIRVANA
Black Berry
Ice
Jock Horror
Kaya
Master Kush
NYPD
Nirvana Special
Raspberry Cough
Swiss Cheese
Urban Poison

The Netherlands
www.nirvana.nl
info@nirvana.nl

PARADISE SEEDS
DelaHaze
Durga Mata
Sativa Spirit
Wappa

The Netherlands
www.paradise-seeds.com
info@paradise-seeds.com

POSITRONICS SEEDS SL
Critical #47

Spain
www.positronicseeds.com
info@positronicseeds.com

REGGAE SEEDS
Dancehall

Spain
www.reggaeseeds.com
info@reggaeseeds.com

RESERVOIR SEEDS
Represented by:
Gypsy Nirvana's
Seed Boutique
Sour Diesel IBL

United Kingdom
www.seedboutique.com
orders@seedboutique.com

SANNIE'S SEEDS
Anesthesia
Herijuana
Killing Fields

The Netherlands
www.sanniesshop.com
whazzup@ns4all.nl

SEEDBANK.COM
Passion Queen

Canada
www.seedbank.com
seedbankdotcom@canada.com

SEEDS OF FREEDOM
Morning Star

Canada
www.seeds-of-freedom.com
seeds-of-freedom@hotmail.com

SENSI SEED BANK
Northern Lights
Northern Lights-Haze

The Netherlands
www.sensiseeds.com
info@sensiseeds.com

SERIOUS SEEDS
AK-47
Kali Mist
White Russian

The Netherlands
www.seriousseeds.com

SOMA SEEDS
Soma A+
Somantra
Soma-licious
New York City Diesel

The Netherlands
www.somaseeds.nl
soma@somaseeds.nl

T.H. SEEDS
A-Train
Burmese Kush
Kushage
MK-Ultra

The Netherlands
www.thseeds.com
info@thseeds.com

TGA SEEDS
Apollo 13BX
Querkle
Sputnik
The Third Dimension

USA
www.tgagenetics.com

Remember, friends don't let friends eat shwag!!!

chebahut.com